W9-CFQ-617

To: _____

From: _____

Dedicated to my precious granddaughters,

Alexis and Jessica.

I look forward to many moments savored with you.

And a big hug and special thank you
to my husband, Michael, my daughter, Michelle,
my editor, Jenny, and my wonderful friends, Nancy, Marsha, and Vicki.
I love you all and I couldn't have done it without you!

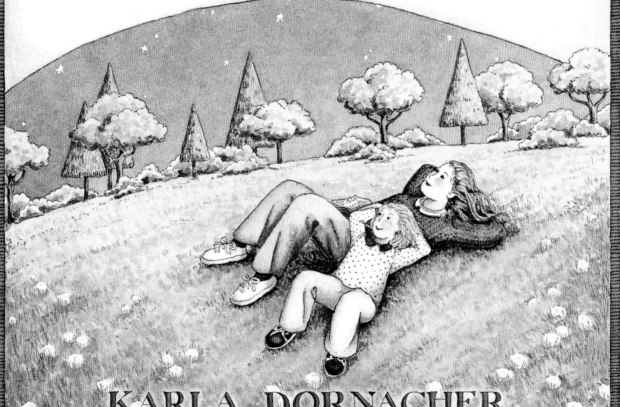

Savor This Moment

Embracing the goodness in everyday life

KARLA DORNACHER

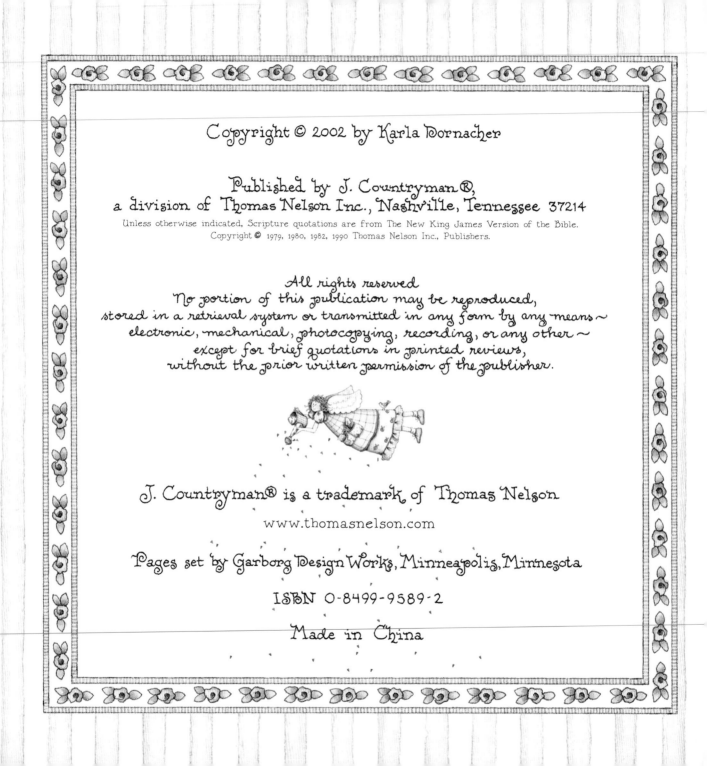

Dear Friend,

Our days are filled, sometimes to overflowing, with what seem to be just ordinary moments. But each moment is a gift from God and a twinkling of time designed to be embraced, employed, and delightfully savored like a delectable piece of chocolate cake, a long hot bath, or a fragrant cup of herbal tea. Oftentimes, those seemingly ordinary moments become amazingly extraordinary when we are able to discover God's presence and design in the midst of them!

For some of us, our lives are so full, we need a reminder on occasion to stop and smell the roses~to catch our breath and refocus on the extraordinary. It is my hope that this little book will encourage you to take the time to reach out . . . or maybe reach within . . . and capture the precious blessings of life that can so easily go unnoticed, lost forever in a whirlwind of busyness.

I pray that you will enjoy this book as much as I have enjoyed writing and illustrating it and that through its pages, your heart will be stirred to savor the moments and enjoy the goodness of everyday life!

May God bless you richly,

Karla

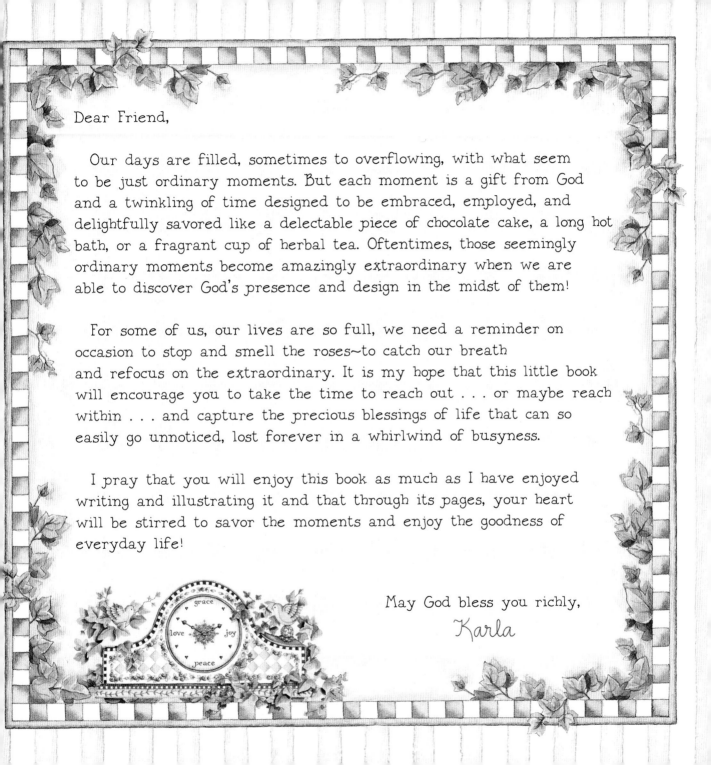

Love ...
bears all things,

believes all things,

hopes all things,

endures all things.

1 Corinthians 13:7

Savor
This Moment
of
Love

Of all the treasures a moment has to offer,
love is the greatest and most priceless jewel of all.
It may sparkle for an instant
in a random act of kindness by a total stranger,
or it may shine for a lifetime
in the golden setting of an intimate relationship.
But above all, it is the most precious gift you can ever receive,
and the most valuable one you can give away.

Unfortunately, our perception of love can so easily become distorted
by rejection, abuse, insensitivity, or unrealistic expectations.
Somewhere along the way, you may come to believe that love
must be earned rather than simply received.
You may even have days when you feel you're not worth loving.

Take heart! I have good news!
Unlike man's love, God's love
is unconditional, and He says you're worth it.
You cannot earn or deserve His love~
you can only open your heart and let it in!
The saying is true:
there is a God~shaped hole in your heart that only He can fill.
So let Him fill it . . . every moment of every day!
Savor His love and then give it away!

And when someone offers the gift to you,
reach out and embrace it with all your heart!

God
has poured out
his love into our hearts
by the Holy Spirit,
whom he has given us.

Romans 5:5, NIV

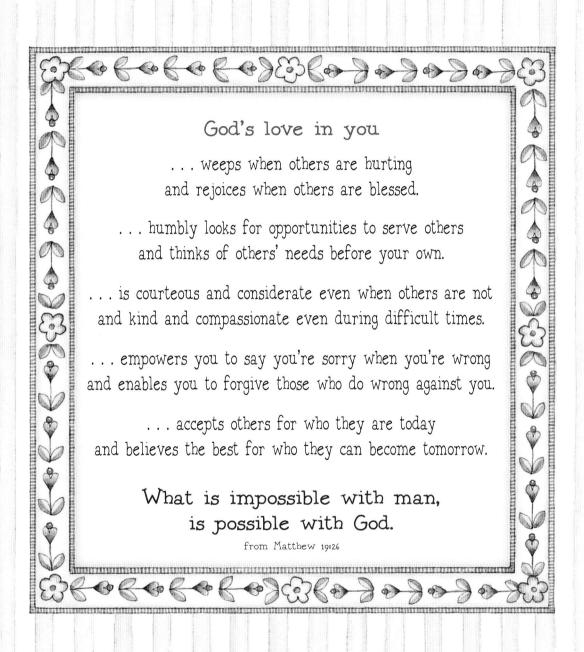

God's love in you

. . . weeps when others are hurting
and rejoices when others are blessed.

. . . humbly looks for opportunities to serve others
and thinks of others' needs before your own.

. . . is courteous and considerate even when others are not
and kind and compassionate even during difficult times.

. . . empowers you to say you're sorry when you're wrong
and enables you to forgive those who do wrong against you.

. . . accepts others for who they are today
and believes the best for who they can become tomorrow.

What is impossible with man,
is possible with God.

from Matthew 19:26

There's a hole in your heart,
an emptiness there,
that longs to be filled
with God's love and care.

You're trying to fill it
with many other things,
not finding the peace
that only Jesus brings.

He longs for you to know
every moment, every day,
His grace is sufficient
and Jesus is the Way.

Only His amazing love
can fill your empty soul.
He died to set you free;
He lives to make you whole.

God wants to hide His truth in your heart today!
Savor this moment.

MY PRAYERS UNTO THEE AND WILL LOOK UP.

MY PRAYERS UNTO THEE AND WILL LOOK UP.

PSALM 5:3

OH LORD; IN THE MORNING I WILL DIRECT

You receive a card in the mail that says,
"My world is a better place . . . thanks to you!"
Your child or grandchild gives you a hug.
Your husband opens the car door for you and, without words,
says, "You are special."
Your boss gives you a raise as a reward for your hard work.

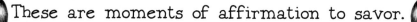 These are moments of affirmation to savor.

These moments reveal our deep need
to feel valued and worthy,
especially in the lives of those we know and love.
But the truth is, they can only touch on our need, not fill it.
Only God can do that.

Your significance is not measured by circumstances, accomplishments,
or the words of other people . . . these things are fickle.
Your true value is determined by God's love
and the truth of who He says you are in His Word.

On those days when there's only junkmail in your mailbox
and your hard work seems taken for granted,
God always has a word of love and affirmation waiting for you.
He says you are a very special person and He should know . . .
He created you!

Savor some moments of affirmation in God's Word today.

You are the apple of God's eye!

from Deuteronomy 32:10

To my Special Daughter

I knew you before you were even born
and there has never been a moment
when I haven't loved you.
I formed you in your mother's womb
and you are precious in my sight.
I created your hands, your heart, your smile ~
and I delight in your beauty.
I have given you gifts, talents, and abilities;
your works are important to me.
You are created in my image
and there is no one else quite like you . . .
YOU ARE SPECIAL!
You are the apple of my eye!

With heavenly hugs,
Your Father
in heaven

Dear Father,

Open my eyes
      that I might see,
the opportunities
      You give to me . . .

To be Your hands,
      Your heart, I pray,
and touch all those
      I see today . . .

With words of love
      and affirmation,
to fill their hearts
      with confirmation . . .

That they might know
      Your love is true
and how very special
      they are to You!

Whatsoever things are lovely...
think on these things. Philippians 4:8

Savor this Moment

Savor
This Moment
of
Gratitude

For three years I lived without running water.
Every few days I would drive to the community hall down the road
and fill a number of five~gallon cans from the outside spigot.
Water for bathing and washing dishes was heated in a large pot on the
stove, and the outhouse was down a path from the back door.

Even though I accepted this inconvenience as part of the experience
and adventure of living in Alaska, I eagerly welcomed the luxury
of indoor plumbing when I moved back to the states.
I can still remember the unspeakable joy I experienced
every time I turned on that faucet and water flowed out!
Whether taking a shower, doing dishes, or just getting a drink,
these were moments I savored with a heart of thanksgiving.

In everything
give thanks

In the routine of everyday life, it's so easy to forget
that the little creature comforts—like running water and electricity—
are a gift from above, a luxury not everyone has.
Now I, like most of us, turn on the tap and expect water to appear.
Still, on occasion, this memory overtakes me and I delight in the moment
. . . a moment of thanksgiving for things so easily taken for granted.

So go ahead, turn on the faucet.
Watch the water flow and savor the moment.
Count your blessings and give thanks.

Like a teapot, filled with His love and power,
God wants to tip you over
and pour out His overflowing grace
on the lives of those around you.

It doesn't matter what your teapot looks like.
You may be short and stout,
or you may be tall and stately.
You may be bright~yellow stoneware with red dots,
or you may be white porcelain with hand~painted roses.

The truth is, no matter what our color or shape,
we're all "cracked pots,"
but God loves us and wants to use us anyway!

Sometimes, however, we get so caught up
worrying about the vessel, we forget all about
the treasure that dwells within us . . .
the love and power of Jesus that is able to influence
our world more than we can even imagine.

Will you ask God to purposely tip you over
and pour you out today?
Offer Him your hands, your heart,
your words, your prayers . . .
then watch who He places along your path!

We have this treasure
in jars of clay
to show that this
all~surpassing power
is from God
and not from us.

2 Corinthians 4:7 NIV

As you humble yourself before My throne
and know that I've called you to be My own,
as you yield your life, your dreams, your plans,
and offer your heart, your voice, your hands,
I'll reveal Myself to you in power ~
moment by moment, hour by hour.

So trust in My love, know it's true,
and the world around you will see Me through you.

I prayed and waited for my husband's salvation for eighteen years.
During that time, the Lord frequently had to remind me
to put my hope and expectation in Jesus—
not in Michael or in myself, but only in Him.
For He alone is able to draw a man to Himself.
It was hope in the Lord—in His love and mercy—
that gave my heart the courage to be patient and persevere.

The Bible tells us that when we pray—
whether for a loved one to know Jesus as Savior and Lord,
for the means to pay next month's bills,
or for whatever our need or heart's desire—
God hears our prayers and is faithful to answer.

Oftentimes, though, the answer does not come right away,
and we go through a period of waiting.
In that season, our faith is tested so our hope must be in God
and the promises of His Word—
not in people or circumstances or the things we can see.

May the eyes of your heart look to the heavens and
be encouraged to endure with joyful expectation.
As you wait for the promise of His blessings to come . . .
savor a moment of hope.

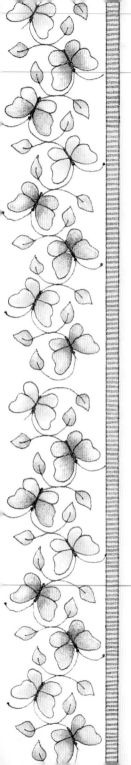

Are you patiently waiting on the Lord?
Or has your faith begun to waver?
Be encouraged, my friend, to persevere,
finding rest and peace in God's favor.

Don't wish upon a shining star
or put your trust in another,
but daily place the cares of your heart
in the hands of your Heavenly Father.

For He has heard your prayers and He knows your heart,
and His answer's a whisper away.
So don't give up, don't doubt His love,
but hold on in faith one more day.

And while you wait, keep your eyes on Jesus.
Let your hope be in Him alone.
Let His Word give light to encourage your soul
and His Spirit give your heart a home.

The Word of God gives birth to faith.
Faith gives wings to hope.
Hope soars high on the promises of God
and gives joy to the soul.

May the God of hope
fill you with all joy and peace
as you trust in Him,
so that you may overflow with hope
by the power of the Holy Spirit.

Romans 15:13 NIV

44

What are you hoping for today?
Write a faith~note to God, thanking Him for hearing your prayers
and acknowledging His promise to answer.

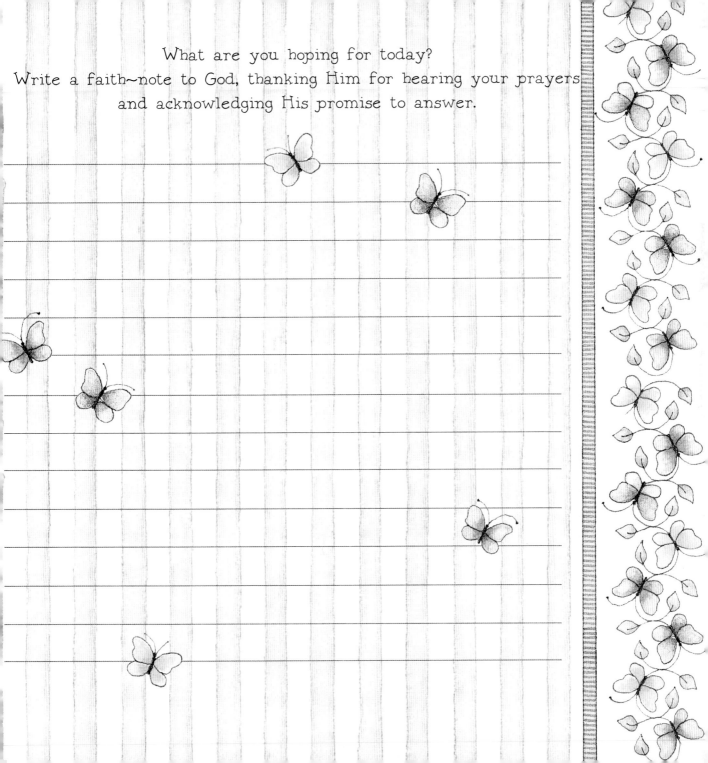

He leads me
beside quiet waters

Psalm 23:2, NIV

Savor
This Moment
of
Rest

Do you have a junk drawer? Most of us do.
Some of us even have cupboards and closets overflowing with clutter~
places so filled with stuff that it's almost impossible
to sort out the "valuables" from the junk.

Just like our drawers and cabinets,
our minds can become so cluttered with activity,
and our thoughts so confused with struggles and stress,
that we lose sight of God
and of what's truly valuable and important in our lives.

You know how to clean out a drawer . . . throw out the junk!
But do you know how to clean out your thoughts?
How do you quiet the worry and fear, the ambition and anxiety?
How do you find rest for your soul?

Moments of rest don't just happen.
Jesus said we should come to Him and He would give us rest.
Ask Him to fill up your mind with thoughts of Himself.
Believe His love to be sovereign over every situation in your life
and His rest will be yours.
(And there will be no room left for all the junk!)

Savor a moment of rest in Jesus today.

My soul finds rest in God alone.

Psalm 62:1, NIV

What am I listening to?
What do I hear?
What are the sounds
that persist in my ear?

Voices from the past
challenge today's expectations,
each one equally loud
and clamoring for attention.

It's a wonder I hear a thing at all
with such noise all around me~
children playing, people talking,
the radio, and the TV!

And then there's the worry,
anxiety, and fear~
they nag and torment with
things I don't want to hear!

Oh Lord, to be quiet~
to hear only Your voice~
is the desire of my heart,
but each day it's a choice.

I can hear You calling
and I know it's true~
I'll find rest for my soul,
as I draw close to You.

Return to your rest,
O my soul
for the Lord has dealt
bountifully with you.

Psalm 116:7

Eight Ways to Savor a Moment of Rest

Take a day, or even an hour, and turn off the phone,
the television, and the radio.
If you're not used to it, it might be difficult to endure at first,
but it will bring peace to your soul.

Read a Psalm a day. It will bring rest your way!

Ponder God's great love.
Count your blessings; name them one by one.

Pray in faith. Give Him all your cares and anxieties!

Take a bubble bath and just rest! Enjoy the quiet.

Take a deep breath, and as you do,
think about how God has filled you with His love.

Take a walk alone and listen for God's still small voice
to whisper in your ear.

Worship the Lord.
Fill your home with praise music and sing along,
or make up a song of your own after reading a Psalm.

Rejoice in the Lord.

Philippians 3:1

Be joyful always.

1 Thessalonians 5:16, NIV

joy

joy

joy

joy

Savor
This Moment
of
Joy

Happy are the people

Psalm 144:15

whose God is the Lord.

I will never forget a story my brother~in~law shared with me.
During one if his well~digging trips to Africa, Jerry met a wonderful
tribe of people. As these natives went about their work,
they suddenly would burst into joyful songs of praise to God.
Their spontaneity surprised Jerry at first, but it became one of the
things he missed the most when he returned home to the states.

Though these people live in remote places, struggling even to survive,
their hearts overflow with joy.
So where, in the midst of their circumstances, does this joy come from?
As I heard this story, it stirred my heart . . . and made me think.

Where does my joy come from?
Am I looking to my circumstances or to my God?
When life all around me seems to be falling apart, when I don't have all the answers or
even know which way to go~

God is with me!
Knowing Him is where my joy comes from.

I want to be a woman who savors moments of joy,
who is so filled up with the joy of knowing Jesus
that periodically it will burst forth from the depth of my being,
like steam from a teakettle, and surprise even me!
Will you join me? And savor this moment of joy!

She who believes in Me...
out of her heart will flow rivers of living water
John 7:38

What can you do today to celebrate
a moment of joy . . .
in your life or in the life of someone you know?

Be joyful.
Be creative.
Be silly.
Be determined.
Be generous.
Be courageous.
Be happy.
Be a blessing.
Be of good cheer.
Be optimistic.
Be thankful.

Believe.

There's joy in working
to hear "job well done,"
joy in cheering
when your child has won.

There's joy in moving
to a better place,
joy in the courage
just to finish the race.

But this joy is fleeting —
here today, gone tomorrow —
and can leave your soul
in terrible sorrow.

For the only true joy
is a gift from above,
that lives in a heart
filled with God's love.

The joy
of the Lord
is your strength.

Nehemiah 8:10

Have you burst into spontaneous joy lately?
If you have, use this space to write about the thought—
or the attitude of your heart—that brought it about.
If you haven't, write a prayer and ask God to cultivate a spirit of joy
within your heart that will surprise even you.

~~~~~~

~~~~~~

~~~~~~

~~~~~~

~~~~~~

~~~~~~

~~~~~~

~~~~~~

~~~~~~

~~~~~~

~~~~~~

~~~~~~

Take a moment and pray for someone you know who needs
the joy of the Lord to fill their lives.

The heavens tell of the glory of God.
The skies display His marvelous craftsmanship.

Psalm 19:1, NLT

Savor
This Moment
of
Beauty

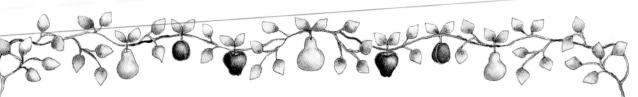

I had read it many times before, but that day it was different.
The words "pleasant to the sight" leapt off the page.
The artist in me smiled to consider that when God planted the very first
garden in Eden, the Bible says He made every tree
pleasant to the sight—as well as good for food.
He wanted to nourish our souls as well as our bodies.

It is God's desire for you to delight in the beauty that surrounds you—
to enjoy the splendor of His handiwork and the glory of His creation.
Trees laden with fruit, birds and flowers,
a rainbow after the storm—
all reminders of God's goodness and grace.

But He also gave you spiritual eyes to behold a beauty
beyond what your natural vision can perceive—
to see and delight in the heart and character of your loving God.
There is no beauty here on earth that can compare to Him.

And as you savor moments in the beauty of His holiness,
you will begin to see the unfading beauty
of a gentle and quiet spirit being formed within you—
the loveliness of a heart inhabited by the love of God,
a beauty that will be seen and enjoyed by all those around you.

Out of the ground
the Lord God made
every tree grow that is
pleasant to the sight
and good for food.

Genesis 2:9

Let the beauty
of the Lord our God
be upon us.

Psalm 90:17

Moments of beauty are gifts from God
to be savored and tucked away,
like snapshots of glorious sunshine
to brighten the bleakest of days.

At a moment when my heart is despairing
and all around me life seems so dim,
I can recall a moment of God's beauty
and refocus my heart on Him.

God painted a rainbow of glory
in the earth and heavens above,
and He has given me eyes to behold it all
by the grace of His mercy and love.

So open my eyes, O God I pray,
to see the butterfly in flight,
to marvel at the smile on a little child's face,
and the stars in the moonlit night.

For beauty is in the eye of the beholder~
Oh Lord, give me eyes to see
and behold the wonder of your great works
and the glory of your majesty!

Look for beauty . . . pursue it.
Keep your eyes open and you may be amazed.

I remember the day someone challenged me to find color in gray clouds.
I thought they were joking. But after a few minutes of intense looking,
I began to see colors I never knew were there.

I challenge you to look for more color in the world around you.
Look up and you will find beauty—in blue skies or gray!

As you walk or drive along a street,
notice all the different shades of greens in the trees and bushes.

Pick a flower—a wildflower—or buy one if you need to.

Find a place to enjoy some fine feathered friends.
Birds are some of God's most beautiful creatures.

Behold a child's face and delight in the beauty of innocence and simplicity.

Ask God to help you see your surroundings
through His eyes and not your own.
Ask Him . . . and then savor the moments!

Bless you ♥

Choose this day to look for God's beauty all around you—
in nature, in people, in your quiet time with God—and savor those
moments. I hope you will find more examples than this page will hold,
but take a moment to write just a few.

Savor
This Moment
of
Comfort

When I see my granddaughter again after a short absence,
I am filled with joy as she runs to me with her arms open wide
and yells, "O Grammy, I missed you so!"

But when she is suffering,
whether from a tumble off of her bike,
a tummy ache, or a broken heart,
it's not Grammy she runs to . . . it's Mommy!

Nothing can compare with a mother's comfort.
Nothing, that is . . . except God's!

The Lord paints a beautiful picture of Himself
and tenderly speaks to our hearts when He says,
"As a mother comforts her child, so will I comfort you."

No matter what your affliction,
no matter what sorrow has beset your spirit,
when you run to God with your broken heart and tear~swollen eyes,
holding out your arms to the Comforter of your soul,
He will never turn you away.
Instead, He reaches down and lifts you up on His knee,
drawing you close to Himself.
And as you sit in the shelter of His arms, embraced by His love,
He will dry your tears and whisper promises of joy to come.

As a mother comforts her child, so will I comfort you.

Isaiah 66:13, NIV

God wants us to be instruments of comfort to one another,
but so often comfort is the most difficult gift to give.
Fear of saying or doing the wrong thing
keeps us from doing anything at all.
So the next time you hesitate,
consider these tried and treasured ways to share the gift of comfort.

Prayer
It can be done any time and anywhere
and should precede any other gifts of comfort!

Food
It nourishes not only the body but also comforts the soul.
Prepare a meal and drop it by~
tape a verse to the dish, such as
"taste and see that the Lord is good" (Psalm 34:8).

Flowers
They reflect God's beauty and bring comfort to the eye.
Pick a bouquet or order one from the florist, if your budget allows.

Snail Mail
There's just something so heartwarming about finding
a note or card in the mail.
Whether you create your own card, buy one,
or just write a note on plain paper,
the message will be appreciated.

Quiet
If you're looking for a way to bring comfort
to someone with small children, offer to take care of her children
for two or three hours or more.

We live in a world that is broken,
filled with suffering and sorrow,
yet God promises to walk with us,
to give us hope to face tomorrow.

In grief or disappointment,
sickness, sin, or deep regret,
God gives us His gift of comfort
to embrace and not forget.

For He sees our tears, hears our prayers,
and knows how deep the pain,
and in the midst of our affliction,
He quietly calls our name.

Like a mother to her child,
He reaches down from above
and gently lifts us in His arms,
embracing our hearts with love.

So if you're feeling broken~hearted,
remember that the Lord is near
to comfort your heart, give you hope,
and dry away every tear.

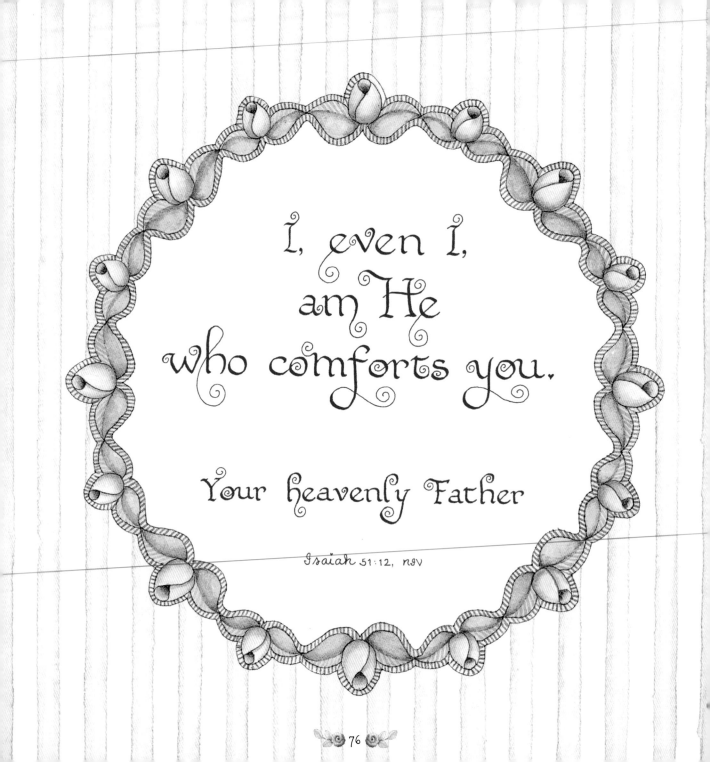

I, even I,
am He
who comforts you.

Your heavenly Father

Isaiah 51:12, nrsv

God is the Father of all compassion and comfort,
and He uses people, like you and me,
to be His heart and hands to those who hurt.
Who are some of the people God has sent
into your life to comfort you?
Take a moment to write a note of thanks
to God for sending them into your life.
And if He leads you to,
you might want to write a note of thanks to them, too.

~~~~~~

~~~~~~

~~~~~~

~~~~~~

~~~~~~

~~~~~~

~~~~~~

~~~~~~

~~~~~~

~~~~~~

~~~~~~

~~~~~~

We don't have to look far to find someone who is suffering.
Would you pray and ask God to show you someone in your
life that needs a touch of the comfort of God through you?

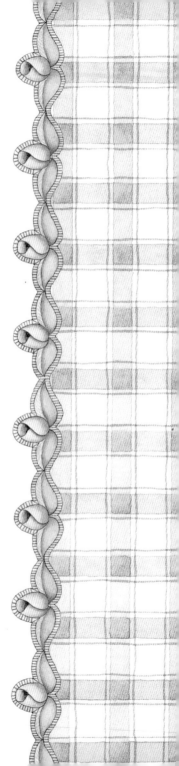

Dear Friend,

Over the past several years, my cup has overflowed with the blessings of the Lord, including the birth of two beautiful granddaughters, a move to the country, and the incredible opportunities I've had to share my faith and love for God through my artwork and writing. These events have filled my life with moments to savor for which I am eternally thankful.

I have learned, however, that there are moments you purposely reach out to embrace, and then there are the moments that reach out and embrace you. One such embracing moment was the catalyst for the title and writing of this book. I was working long hours, totally absorbed in trying to meet the deadline for my last book when I heard a little voice, as if it were real, saying, *Yes, that was my Grandma, but she was so busy I never really knew her.* In that moment, God touched my heart and changed my life. "Savor this Moment" became my motto, and I have since become determined to live my life more carefully and embrace the moments that really count!

Our lives are fleeting—in the same instance a moment appears, it is gone again, never to return. Will you join with me in purposely reaching out and grasping hold of the precious moments of everyday life? As you do, may you encounter the divine love of God in every one of them.

May the Lord bless you and keep you,
Karla Dornacher

This little angel is a reflection of your heart
as you pour out, through your words and deeds,
the love of God into the lives of those around you.

Will you pour out a splash of God's love today by sending this postcard
with a note of encouragement to someone you know and care about?
Give them a moment to savor!

I would also be blessed and encouraged by hearing from you~
to know your response to the stories, art, and verses in this little book.
Did you find comfort for your soul?
Did you gain new insight into some ordinary moments?
Were you reminded of moments of your own?

Capture a moment and send it with a prayer to~
Karla Dornacher ✿ P.O. Box 185 ✿ Battle Ground, WA 98604
Use this postcard, pen a letter, or visit me on the web at:
www.karladornacher.com

Other books from my heart and hand . . .

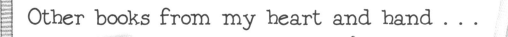

Love In Every Room

A walk through a very special house where, room by room, you will be encouraged as a woman of God—and as the keeper of your home. Excellent gift for a housewarming party, bridal shower, or wedding, or just to encourage a woman's heart.

Down A Garden Path

Stroll down the path of a very special garden and pause along the way to let God till the soil of your heart, and plant a few seeds of faith. As you read, yield to a bit of divine pruning, or sit in the shade and simply enjoy the presence of the Lord. This gift book is not for your gardening friends only, but for any woman desiring to grow in her faith and walk with the Master Gardener of her soul. Great for new believers and seekers too.

The Blessing of Friendship

Designed to celebrate the gift of friendship, both with Jesus and with other women, this book encourages us to look at the depth and the delights of embracing godly friendships. It includes several journaling pages, which make it an ideal gift to bless and encourage the women friends in your life.

More of my books available from J. Countryman® include: *A Daily Agenda* calendar book, the *I Celebrate You* greeting~card book, and *A Box of Blessings*, a collection of small cards with a million uses. Great gifts for yourself or to give away!